ALEXA PLUS(+)
What Is It All About?

*How Amazon's Bold Upgrade Is Shaping
the Future of Personal Assistance—and
Why You Should Care*

Jackson Z. Scott

Table of Contents

Introduction:... 3

Chapter 1: The Rise of Alexa—From Basic Assistant to Smart Personal Assistant..7

Chapter 2: The Power of Alexa Plus (+) – How It Works...15

Chapter 3: The Personal Touch – Alexa Plus Can Remember and Understand You.............................. 26

Chapter 4: Alexa Plus in Your Smart Home – Seamlessly Integrating Into Your Life...................... 38

Chapter 5: Alexa Plus for Everyday Use – Helping with the Little Things...51

Chapter 6: The Future of Alexa – What's Next for AI and Personal Assistance... 62

Chapter 7: Pricing and Availability – What You Need to Know.. 75

Chapter 8: The Pros and Cons of Alexa Plus – Is It Worth the Price?... 83

Chapter 9: A Look at the Competitors – How Does Alexa Plus Stack Up?...93

Conclusion.. 102

Introduction:

Amazon has always been at the forefront of revolutionizing the way we interact with technology. From the moment Alexa made her debut, it was clear that voice-activated assistants were changing the way we communicated with devices. But Alexa Plus is taking this transformation a step further, ushering in a new era for smart assistants. Gone are the days when Alexa simply responded to commands like setting a timer or checking the weather. Now, Alexa Plus is far more sophisticated, turning from a basic assistant into a deeply intelligent, context-aware personal helper that understands your preferences, helps you plan your day, and even looks out for your security.

The upgrade is not just an evolution—it's a massive leap forward. Alexa Plus is powered by cutting-edge AI, combining Amazon's own large language model (LLM) technology with advanced generative AI models, including Claude from Anthropic. The result? A virtual assistant that doesn't just answer questions but engages in nuanced conversations, remembers your routines, and offers relevant suggestions without you needing to repeat yourself. This transformation elevates Alexa beyond a simple voice interface and integrates her deeper into your daily life, becoming a more proactive, almost human-like presence in your home.

This shift marks a pivotal point in the future of personal assistance, with the potential to redefine how we interact with technology. The new Alexa isn't just a tool for answering queries—it's a companion that can anticipate your needs and make your life more streamlined and organized. Alexa Plus takes on complex tasks that were once the domain of specialized apps or even human assistants, allowing users to delegate more and more responsibilities to their voice assistant. Whether it's planning a family dinner, managing your home security, or handling your schedule, Alexa Plus is stepping into the role of an intelligent personal assistant that keeps track of your preferences and needs, offering a tailored experience.

The growing integration of artificial intelligence into our homes is more than just a trend—it's a glimpse into the future of how we will live, work, and interact with the world around us. The home assistant is no longer just an interactive gadget; it's evolving into a hub of personal efficiency, integrating seamlessly with other smart devices. And amid all the new smart assistants entering the market, Alexa Plus stands out, not only because of its deep learning capabilities but because it brings this level of intelligence into the home at an accessible price point, especially for Amazon Prime members.

As we look to the future, the question becomes: how will Alexa Plus change the way we live, work, and even interact with each other? The possibilities are limitless, and as this technology continues to grow, it will undoubtedly pave the way for even smarter, more intuitive systems that adapt and evolve alongside us. But before diving into the specifics of what Alexa Plus can do, it's essential to understand what makes this upgrade so special and how it differs from its predecessors.

Chapter 1: The Rise of Alexa—From Basic Assistant to Smart Personal Assistant

Alexa's journey began as a simple, yet revolutionary concept: a voice assistant that could answer basic questions and perform simple tasks through voice commands. When Amazon introduced the Echo device in 2014, many were intrigued by the idea of having a virtual assistant right in their homes. At the time, Alexa's capabilities were modest. She could set timers, play music, provide weather updates, and answer questions like, "What's the capital of France?" and "What time is it in Tokyo?" These basic tasks formed the core of Alexa's early appeal, making it a convenient tool for those who needed a hands-free solution for everyday inquiries.

The initial version of Alexa was designed to be a voice-activated assistant that could enhance convenience, but its real potential wasn't immediately clear. Alexa's simplicity was both its strength and limitation. People were amazed that they could ask questions and get instant responses, all without lifting a finger. But beyond these simple queries, Alexa's functionality remained relatively limited, catering mostly to entertainment and everyday questions.

However, it didn't take long for Amazon to see the potential for growth in this space. As the smart home revolution started to take shape, Amazon realized Alexa could play a pivotal role in the emerging landscape of connected devices. So, Alexa's next evolution was a leap into the world of smart home control.

Over time, Amazon expanded Alexa's functionality to allow users to control lights, thermostats, security systems, and other smart devices in their homes. With the integration of third-party products, Alexa became the central hub for home automation, able to adjust temperatures, turn off lights, lock doors, and even monitor security cameras, all with a simple voice command. This expansion turned Alexa from a basic voice assistant into a smart home platform—a tool that could manage multiple devices and orchestrate complex tasks across a wide range of devices from different manufacturers.

This marked a critical turning point in Alexa's evolution, as she began to take on a more central role in the household, transforming from a curious gadget into a central command hub for smart homes. Alexa was no longer just a voice assistant for answering questions; she became an essential part of modern living, connecting everything from lights and locks to refrigerators and coffee machines, helping create a fully automated and integrated home experience.

But despite these advancements, Alexa still had limitations. The AI was rule-based and lacked the deeper understanding and context that would allow for more nuanced, intelligent interactions. While it was impressive to tell Alexa to "turn off the living room lights" or "set the thermostat to 72°F," there was still a sense of disconnection—a gap between user expectations and Alexa's ability to handle more complex, dynamic tasks. What was missing was the intelligence to understand context, remember personal preferences, and anticipate needs.

This brings us to the current evolution—Alexa Plus. With the integration of advanced AI and large language models, Alexa has gone from a useful assistant for household control to a highly intelligent, context-aware personal assistant. And this transition is changing everything.

As technology has progressed, so have the expectations of users. When Alexa was first introduced, it was nothing short of groundbreaking. The ability to interact with a device simply by using voice commands was a leap forward in convenience and accessibility. But as the years passed, it became increasingly clear that Alexa's capabilities were no longer enough to keep up with the rapid pace of technological advancement.

Consumers began to demand more. They wanted an assistant that could do more than just play music or check the weather. They desired a smarter, more intuitive system that could understand the context of conversations, recall personal preferences, and handle increasingly complex tasks with ease. In short, the world had moved on from the novelty of voice commands; people now wanted an intelligent assistant that could anticipate their needs, solve problems, and provide a more personalized experience.

For Amazon, this shift in consumer expectations was an opportunity—and a necessity. If Alexa was to maintain its relevance in a growing field of AI-driven personal assistants, Amazon had to innovate. The landscape of voice assistants was becoming more competitive, with companies like Google and Apple making significant strides in AI and machine learning. Alexa needed to evolve from being a simple voice command system to a more dynamic, intelligent assistant capable of understanding and adapting to the nuances of daily life.

This is where Alexa Plus comes in. The need for an upgrade became evident as Amazon recognized that Alexa's basic functionality no longer met the growing demands of its users. It was time to take Alexa to the next level, to transform it from a useful, albeit limited, assistant into a truly intelligent, context-aware entity capable of providing a deeper, more meaningful interaction.

Alexa Plus leverages generative AI and large language models (LLMs)—the cutting-edge technology driving the latest advancements in AI. These models allow Alexa to process information in a more human-like way, understanding not only the literal meaning of words but also the context behind them. With generative AI, Alexa can engage in more nuanced conversations, follow up on previous discussions, and retain context across multiple interactions. This transformation empowers Alexa to take on tasks that were once outside its reach—like remembering personal preferences, suggesting activities based on your schedule, or even making decisions based on a deeper understanding of your life.

Large language models, such as those powered by Anthropic's Claude and Amazon's own Bedrock platform, enable Alexa Plus to hold more sophisticated conversations, allowing it to go beyond basic commands. It becomes capable of learning and adapting to your needs, creating a more personalized experience that is informed by past interactions. Whether it's planning your day, assisting with family meals, or even managing your home security, Alexa Plus isn't just responding to commands—it's anticipating them, ensuring a seamless and tailored experience for each user.

In essence, Alexa Plus represents Amazon's response to the growing need for smarter, more capable personal assistants. It is the company's bold move to transform Alexa into something more than just a voice in your home—it's an intelligent partner, a proactive assistant that can simplify your life, manage your tasks, and enhance your overall experience with the growing ecosystem of smart devices. This upgrade is about making Alexa more than just a tool—it's about making her an essential part of your daily life.

Chapter 2: The Power of Alexa Plus (+) – How It Works

The difference between the regular Alexa and Alexa Plus is more than just an update in the user interface or added features. It's a fundamental shift in how the assistant operates, powered by advancements in artificial intelligence and machine learning. While both Alexa and Alexa Plus are designed to simplify tasks and manage smart home systems, Alexa Plus is a game-changer in the realm of voice assistants.

One of the key differentiators is the integration of Claude, an advanced AI model developed by Anthropic, along with Amazon's own AI technologies built through the Bedrock platform. Regular Alexa operates on a relatively simpler framework that relies heavily on predefined responses and set rules to handle voice commands. While this system is effective for basic tasks—playing music, setting reminders, or controlling smart home devices—it often struggles with more complex interactions or maintaining context across different conversations. This is where Alexa Plus steps in.

By incorporating Claude and Bedrock's AI capabilities, Alexa Plus now utilizes large language models (LLMs) to vastly improve its ability to understand language in a more nuanced, human-like manner. LLMs are a type of AI that can process and generate language that mimics natural conversation. Unlike traditional models, which are based on rigid scripts and patterns, LLMs can interpret words and phrases based on context, tone, and the flow of an ongoing conversation. This makes Alexa Plus much more capable of understanding not just the literal meaning of what you say, but the underlying context behind it.

One of the most impressive advancements in Alexa Plus is its contextual understanding. With regular Alexa, if you asked her to play a song, then later asked her to set a reminder, she might not be able to link the two interactions. But Alexa Plus, with its use of LLMs, can keep track of prior requests and tie them together seamlessly. This allows Alexa to better understand what you're asking, even if it's a follow-up or a more complicated request that requires knowledge of earlier interactions.

In addition to improved context, Alexa Plus also introduces memory, allowing the assistant to remember personal details and preferences across sessions. This memory allows for a more personalized experience. For instance, if you tell Alexa you're vegetarian, Alexa Plus will remember that next time you're planning a meal and can suggest recipes that align with your dietary preferences. Similarly, if you mention that your partner is allergic to gluten or that your kids love pizza, Alexa Plus will tailor future suggestions accordingly. This level of personalization is something the regular Alexa, without its memory and contextual abilities, can't offer.

Another major upgrade in Alexa Plus is its ability to handle more complex, nuanced conversations. With the integration of Claude and large language models, Alexa Plus can engage in multi-turn conversations that flow naturally. Whereas regular Alexa might require you to repeat commands or clarify your requests multiple times, Alexa Plus can follow along, remember details, and adapt its responses in real time. For example, if you mention you're planning a music-themed party, Alexa Plus might follow up by helping you create a shopping list, suggest a playlist, and even order party supplies, all while maintaining the context of the ongoing conversation.

Moreover, Alexa Plus's integration with generative AI makes it capable of understanding and acting on more complex tasks. If you ask Alexa Plus to summarize a lengthy document or help you study for an exam, it can break down the content into easily digestible pieces, creating bullet points or quiz questions tailored to your needs. This is another area where Alexa Plus outshines the regular

Alexa, whose capabilities are limited to basic voice responses and static commands.

In terms of overall functionality, Alexa Plus offers a much deeper and more sophisticated level of interaction. While the regular Alexa can still perform essential tasks and control smart devices, it lacks the ability to personalize interactions, recall previous conversations, and seamlessly integrate with various external platforms and services. Alexa Plus, with its generative AI and LLMs, creates a more immersive, intelligent, and responsive experience, bringing voice assistants into the next generation of AI-powered technology.

In short, the jump from regular Alexa to Alexa Plus is like going from a simple, reliable tool to an intelligent partner capable of understanding the intricacies of your daily life. The inclusion of Claude's AI technology and Amazon's own cutting-edge LLMs makes Alexa Plus not just a better assistant—it makes it a smarter, more intuitive presence in your home, anticipating your needs and handling complex tasks with ease.

Generative AI is a powerful form of artificial intelligence that goes beyond simply responding to user commands; it can create new, meaningful outputs based on the data and information it processes. This AI technology enables Alexa Plus to perform tasks that were once out of reach for traditional voice assistants. Unlike regular AI, which typically follows a pre-programmed script or set of rules, generative AI has the ability to understand context, adapt to new situations, and even generate content, responses, or solutions in real time.

At its core, generative AI uses large language models (LLMs) to simulate a deep understanding of language, making it capable of crafting original responses, suggesting ideas, and performing tasks that are nuanced and personalized. This allows Alexa Plus to do more than just read back information or follow basic voice commands—it can engage in intelligent, context-aware conversations and seamlessly perform complex, multi-step tasks.

One of the standout features of Alexa Plus powered by generative AI is its conversational memory. While regular Alexa can respond to a command, it has limited memory and context awareness. If you tell it something, like, "I'm vegetarian," and ask for a dinner recipe later, Alexa won't remember that you prefer plant-based meals. Alexa Plus, however, can retain that information over time, allowing it to recall your preferences, habits, and details you've shared. This memory lets Alexa Plus create more meaningful, tailored suggestions based on your past interactions.

Take, for example, planning a meal. If you mention that you're hosting a dinner party for a group of friends and that you're vegetarian, Alexa Plus can remember that detail from previous conversations. When you ask for a recipe, it won't just suggest any dish—it'll recommend something that fits your dietary needs, possibly even considering your friends' preferences if you've shared that information before. This type of personalized planning isn't just a convenience; it transforms Alexa Plus into a more proactive, intelligent assistant capable of anticipating your needs.

Conversational memory also extends to everyday tasks. Suppose you ask Alexa Plus to set a reminder to buy groceries. Later in the week, if you mention that you're having guests over, Alexa Plus can recall your shopping list and help you plan a menu or suggest additional items. Instead of needing to manually update your list or repeat information, Alexa Plus automatically adapts and tailors its assistance to the evolving needs of the user, turning what would traditionally be a static interaction into a dynamic, ongoing relationship.

Another example of how generative AI enhances Alexa Plus's abilities is through contextual awareness. Unlike traditional assistants, which rely on a rigid sequence of commands, Alexa Plus understands context and can follow along in multi-turn conversations. For instance, if you're discussing a party theme, Alexa Plus can help with planning logistics, ordering groceries, creating a music playlist, and even sending out invitations—all while maintaining awareness of the ongoing context. It can pick up where the conversation left off, remembering relevant details without needing constant reminders.

Imagine telling Alexa Plus that you're organizing a music-themed party. The assistant might ask, "What kind of music are you thinking of?" and, after you answer, continue by suggesting a playlist, ordering supplies, and even scheduling delivery times. Alexa Plus's ability to hold onto the context of the conversation, even across different tasks, makes it feel more like a personal assistant rather than a machine following a checklist.

Generative AI also enables Alexa Plus to handle more complex requests. If you're working on a big project, such as preparing for an important presentation, you can upload documents and ask

Alexa Plus to summarize the key points or even quiz you on the material. This goes far beyond what regular Alexa could do, which would typically just fetch the document or offer limited information. With Alexa Plus, generative AI helps you engage deeply with the content by breaking it down into easy-to-understand summaries or by asking you questions that help reinforce your learning. This integration of AI and learning tools creates a more interactive and tailored experience that empowers you to be more productive.

Furthermore, Alexa Plus can assist in analyzing media or photos. If you're at the grocery store and need to check your fridge for a particular item, Alexa Plus could analyze a picture of your refrigerator and notify you whether you're low on specific ingredients, making your shopping experience even more efficient.

In summary, the integration of generative AI into Alexa Plus is what sets it apart from basic assistants. This technology not only enables Alexa

Plus to remember information, plan and perform complex tasks, and maintain contextual understanding, but it also gives it the ability to evolve and adapt based on each unique interaction. It's a massive leap forward in terms of making Alexa a genuinely intelligent, context-aware personal assistant—one that doesn't just respond to commands, but understands the bigger picture and helps users navigate their day in a more intuitive and personalized way.

Chapter 3: The Personal Touch – Alexa Plus Can Remember and Understand You

One of the most powerful and game-changing features of Alexa Plus is its memory function, which enables the assistant to remember your personal preferences, habits, and even details about your schedule. This feature represents a giant leap forward from the more basic Alexa, which typically forgets everything after a session ends. With Alexa Plus, your preferences and daily routines are stored in its memory, allowing it to continuously improve and personalize its assistance over time.

Imagine waking up on a typical morning. You ask Alexa to play your favorite playlist, and without having to give a command each time, it knows exactly which genre or artist you like to hear in the mornings. Later in the day, Alexa recalls that you prefer light snacks, so when you ask for a suggestion, it will offer healthier, plant-based options—without you needing to specify. This is just one example of how Alexa Plus takes personalization to the next level by remembering things that matter to you, which creates a seamless, intelligent experience.

The ability to remember specific preferences can also help with more practical tasks like meal planning. Suppose you're vegetarian or have specific dietary restrictions, like avoiding gluten. With Alexa Plus's memory, you don't have to repeat this information every time you ask for a recipe or grocery list. Alexa Plus will automatically consider your dietary needs when offering suggestions. For instance, if you ask for dinner ideas, Alexa will offer vegetarian recipes and avoid suggesting meals with gluten, all without needing to ask for this detail repeatedly.

The same memory function can also be applied to family and household preferences. If you've mentioned that your partner is gluten-free or has a nut allergy, Alexa Plus can keep this information in mind for future meal plans or shopping lists. If you're preparing a family meal, Alexa can suggest recipes that cater to everyone's dietary needs, ensuring that it doesn't recommend any ingredients that might trigger an allergy or cause discomfort for a family member.

Let's consider a more concrete example: you and your partner decide to host a dinner party, and you've mentioned a few details to Alexa during earlier conversations. When it's time to plan the menu, Alexa remembers both of your preferences. If you've told it that you love Mediterranean dishes while your partner prefers gluten-free food, Alexa can recommend a variety of Mediterranean recipes that are naturally gluten-free, or it might suggest alternatives to dishes that contain gluten. This level of tailored assistance makes meal planning easier, more convenient, and less stressful, freeing you up to focus on enjoying the moment instead of worrying about details.

Even more impressive, Alexa Plus doesn't just stop at remembering dietary preferences—it can also recall your schedule and integrate it with other tasks. If you've told Alexa that you work out every morning at 6 a.m. or that you have a recurring weekly meeting on Thursday afternoons, it can remind you of these activities automatically. For example, if you ask Alexa to recommend a new healthy snack for your post-workout routine, it can suggest something that aligns with your dietary preferences, knowing that you're likely looking for something to fuel your fitness goals.

This personalization extends to lifestyle choices as well. For example, if you mention that you prefer a minimalist home or that you're looking to simplify your life, Alexa Plus can recommend products, services, and strategies that align with these preferences. Similarly, if you mention that you're exploring new hobbies, like learning to play the guitar, Alexa might suggest related lessons or activities, making the assistant more than just a tool—it becomes a partner in helping you grow and pursue your interests.

What truly sets this memory feature apart is its adaptability. As Alexa Plus learns more about you over time, it adjusts its responses and suggestions based on your evolving preferences. This means that as you change your routines, adopt new habits, or discover new interests, Alexa Plus will be right there with you, offering support and guidance that is always in sync with where you are in life.

For instance, let's say you move to a new city, and your eating habits change because you're now exposed to new ingredients or cultural influences. Alexa Plus, over time, can learn these changes and begin suggesting meals and recipes that reflect your new environment and lifestyle. It doesn't just recall old information—it adapts to new circumstances, making it incredibly dynamic and responsive.

This level of personalization isn't just limited to food and fitness. It extends to the entire range of tasks you interact with on a daily basis—whether it's managing your calendar, controlling your smart home devices, or even suggesting new entertainment based on your mood and preferences. It feels as though Alexa Plus is always in tune with your life, evolving right along with you and making your day-to-day activities easier and more enjoyable.

In short, the memory function of Alexa Plus is a game-changer. By remembering your preferences, dietary restrictions, schedules, and personal details, it creates an assistant that feels less like a tool and more like a trusted partner who understands you. Whether you're managing your home, planning a meal, or organizing your life, Alexa Plus's ability to tailor its responses and actions to your individual needs ensures that it's always working in the background to make your life smoother and more efficient.

Alexa Plus takes personal assistance far beyond the realm of simple commands by harnessing the power of memory to proactively suggest, manage, and automate various aspects of your daily life. With its advanced memory capabilities, Alexa Plus can remember not just your preferences but also anticipate your needs, saving you time and effort in ways that go well beyond what you may have imagined a virtual assistant could do.

For example, imagine it's the weekend, and you're in the mood to cook something new for dinner. Rather than asking Alexa for specific recipe suggestions, you can simply ask for dinner ideas, and Alexa will tailor its suggestions based on what it remembers about your past preferences and dietary restrictions. Maybe you've told it that you love Italian cuisine, or that you avoid dairy. Alexa will keep these in mind and suggest recipes that fit your tastes. Even better, it can retrieve ingredients from your kitchen inventory and cross-reference them with the recipe, making it even easier to start cooking without needing to go to the store.

Let's say you've had a busy week and are looking to unwind with a night out. Alexa Plus, drawing on your memory, could suggest a restaurant that you've enjoyed in the past or recommend a new spot based on what it knows you like. With Alexa Plus's integrations with services like OpenTable, it can even go a step further and make a reservation for you, automatically securing a spot without you needing to provide all the details. No need to go through the hassle of searching for available tables or calling the restaurant—you can rely on Alexa to handle the reservation seamlessly.

What about when you're too busy to cook or don't feel like going to the grocery store? Alexa Plus is not just a virtual assistant that remembers your preferences, but also one that integrates with other services to make life even easier. If you regularly order groceries or food delivery, Alexa can suggest items based on your past purchases or current needs. For example, it might recognize that you're running low on fresh produce or that you've been ordering certain items weekly and will prompt you to reorder them. It can even place the order on your behalf, taking care of the details while you get on with your day.

Alexa Plus's integrations with Amazon services such as Amazon Music also add another layer of convenience. If you enjoy listening to specific playlists or genres during certain activities, Alexa can automatically queue up music that aligns with your mood, whether it's upbeat tracks for a workout or relaxing melodies for winding down at night. If you've mentioned that you love podcasts or audiobooks, Alexa can offer recommendations based on your listening habits, creating an atmosphere tailored to whatever you're doing at the moment.

This integration goes beyond just Amazon. Alexa Plus connects with third-party services to create an even more seamless experience. Whether it's using OpenTable for reservations, checking traffic updates through Google Maps, or even controlling smart home devices like thermostats or lights through other platforms, Alexa's ability to remember and integrate with a variety of services means it's always prepared to make your life easier.

Alexa Plus also understands the concept of context, further enhancing its ability to respond appropriately. Let's say it's the holiday season, and you've previously told Alexa that you prefer hosting family gatherings or that you always travel to visit relatives. Based on this information, Alexa could not only suggest holiday recipes but also remind you to pick up specific items for the event or help with finding gift ideas. It can remember the special touches you like to include during celebrations, and suggest ways to make your gatherings even more enjoyable. When you're preparing for a big family dinner, Alexa might even offer a full menu suggestion based on what it knows you've enjoyed in the past, eliminating the need for you to brainstorm on your own.

Similarly, if you've been working on a project or have a deadline coming up, Alexa might offer to set reminders, find resources, or suggest tools that could help. It might even draft out an email for you, summarizing information that's relevant to the task you're working on—without you having to ask for every step individually. As Alexa becomes more integrated into your day-to-day life, these seemingly small tasks add up to a huge time-saving benefit, freeing you from constant manual organization and helping you focus on the things that matter most.

This type of proactive assistance is a direct result of Alexa Plus's enhanced capabilities. Instead of waiting for a command, Alexa Plus anticipates your needs and takes the initiative to make suggestions, make plans, and execute tasks—all based on its memory of your preferences, habits, and context. It's an intelligent assistant that evolves alongside you, becoming more intuitive and responsive over time.

In addition to being able to help with daily tasks, Alexa Plus also acts as a "central hub" for your connected life, managing everything from your entertainment preferences to your home automation, all by remembering what you like and need. It can act as your personal assistant, concierge, and even your personal shopper—offering solutions and carrying out tasks in a way that seems almost magical.

In short, Alexa Plus goes beyond simply responding to commands. It anticipates needs, makes suggestions, and proactively handles tasks that would otherwise take up your time. With its integrations into third-party services, such as OpenTable, Amazon Music, and more, it truly becomes an all-in-one assistant that's as intelligent as it is convenient. Whether it's ordering groceries, making reservations, or creating personalized playlists, Alexa Plus is constantly working in the background to ensure that your life is as smooth and effortless as possible. It's no longer just a tool—it's a true partner in your daily routine.

Chapter 4: Alexa Plus in Your Smart Home – Seamlessly Integrating Into Your Life

Alexa Plus's integration with home devices takes the concept of a "smart home" to an entirely new level. By leveraging its advanced AI capabilities, Alexa Plus seamlessly connects with various smart home gadgets, including Echo devices, Ring security cameras, smart thermostats, and more. This integration allows Alexa to act as the central hub that manages your home, providing both convenience and peace of mind.

When you step into a home powered by Alexa Plus, it's like having an intelligent assistant that is always on hand to ensure everything runs smoothly. Imagine arriving home after a long day and asking Alexa to turn on the lights and adjust the thermostat to your preferred temperature—all without lifting a finger. Thanks to Alexa's integration with devices like smart thermostats, lights, and fans, your home can be automatically set up to your liking before you even step through the door. You can even control multiple devices at once with just a simple voice command, creating an environment that feels just right.

For those concerned with home security, Alexa Plus offers a whole new level of convenience and peace of mind. Integration with Ring security cameras and other smart security devices means that Alexa can actively monitor the perimeter of your home and alert you about any unusual activity. Suppose someone rings your doorbell, Alexa can show you a live video feed from the Ring camera right on your Echo Show or smart display, giving you a clear view of who's at the door, whether you're home or away. You can even respond to the visitor without opening the door, using Alexa's built-in two-way communication.

This security integration goes even further by allowing Alexa to arm and disarm security systems, manage surveillance cameras, and even lock doors with simple voice commands. For example, if you're at the grocery store and want to make sure everything is secure at home, you can ask Alexa to check the status of your security system or remind you to lock the doors. If you're out of town on vacation, Alexa can provide you with regular security updates, making it feel like your home is always being actively monitored, even when you're not there.

When it comes to deliveries, Alexa Plus offers another layer of convenience. Integration with Amazon's delivery services and Ring doorbell systems means that you can check the status of your packages in real-time. Alexa can notify you when a delivery is made, and if you have a Ring camera, it can show you a live feed of the delivery as it happens. If you're expecting multiple packages, Alexa will keep you updated on each one's progress, ensuring that you never miss a delivery.

For those with pets, Alexa Plus can even step in as an extra set of eyes. Imagine you're out for the day, and you're wondering what your pet is up to at home. With cameras like the Ring Pet Camera or other pet-monitoring devices, Alexa can show you a live video feed of your furry friends in real-time. It can also alert you if your pet is acting out of the ordinary, such as getting into something they shouldn't or barking excessively. This integration gives pet owners peace of mind, knowing they can check on their pets from anywhere, anytime.

In the evening, as you prepare for bed, Alexa Plus can help wrap up your day by making sure everything is in order. It can check that your lights are off, your security cameras are active, and your doors are locked. If you've forgotten to set the alarm or turn off a device, Alexa will remind you and allow you to make adjustments on the spot, ensuring that you're always one step ahead when it comes to home management.

Alexa Plus also provides a way to stay on top of your home's energy consumption. Integration with smart thermostats like the Nest or Ecobee allows you to monitor and adjust the temperature in your home with ease. During the day, Alexa can ensure that your thermostat is set to energy-saving levels when you're away, and then automatically adjust it for comfort when you return home. You can even check the temperature from your phone, making it easy to ensure you're saving energy without sacrificing comfort.

One of the most convenient features of Alexa Plus's home integration is its ability to automate everyday tasks based on your routines. Alexa can learn your daily habits—when you wake up, when you leave the house, when you get home—and adjust settings accordingly. For example, in the morning, Alexa might automatically adjust the thermostat to your desired temperature, turn on the lights, and start playing your favorite music to help you start the day. In the evening, it might dim the lights, turn off any unnecessary devices, and activate your security system, all based on your set routines.

This seamless connectivity with home devices doesn't just stop at comfort and convenience; it plays a key role in improving the overall safety and security of your home. Alexa Plus can act as a personal assistant that proactively manages your home environment, from adjusting temperatures to ensuring everything is locked up and secure. With its intuitive AI capabilities, Alexa Plus can anticipate what you need and manage everything in the background, leaving you free to focus on what matters most.

In essence, Alexa Plus is more than just an assistant; it is a smart home manager that integrates every aspect of your home's devices into one cohesive, intelligent system. It brings together all the various parts of your smart home, from security to entertainment to energy management, creating a central hub that not only simplifies your life but also enhances your home's functionality. By being able to manage and monitor everything with ease, Alexa Plus ensures that your home is always secure, comfortable, and running efficiently—no matter where you are.

As Alexa becomes more integrated into our lives and homes, it's natural to have concerns about privacy and how much personal information is being shared or stored. The more connected and intelligent our devices become, the more questions arise about how much data they're collecting and how it is being used. Alexa Plus, with its advanced AI capabilities, is no different. The potential for deeper data collection—whether it's remembering preferences, understanding your routines, or processing sensitive conversations—raises valid concerns about the safety and privacy of users.

Amazon, fully aware of these concerns, has put considerable effort into addressing them. As Alexa evolves, the company has made several important strides in ensuring that users can still enjoy the benefits of this powerful AI assistant while maintaining control over their personal data.

One of the key features Amazon has implemented is encryption. All communications with Alexa, whether it's a simple voice command or a more complex interaction involving personal information, are encrypted to protect against unauthorized access. This means that when you ask Alexa Plus about your schedule, request a grocery order, or set up a reminder for an event, your data is safely encrypted during transmission, making it difficult for anyone to intercept or misuse that information. Encryption ensures that your personal conversations and data are kept secure and confidential.

In addition to encryption, Amazon has also introduced local processing for certain types of interactions. This means that not all data needs to leave your device to be processed. Some requests can be handled directly on the Echo device itself, without being sent to Amazon's servers. For example, when you issue a simple command like turning off the lights, Alexa can handle this request locally, meaning that no sensitive information is transmitted to external servers. By keeping certain processing tasks local, Amazon reduces the risk of data exposure and improves the overall security of the system.

Amazon has also launched a new privacy dashboard, giving users greater control and transparency over the data being collected. This dashboard allows you to review your voice recordings, see what data Alexa has stored, and delete any information you no longer want Alexa to retain. This feature is particularly useful for users who may have concerns about their interactions with Alexa being stored for extended periods. Through the privacy dashboard, you can easily manage your voice history, delete recordings, or even set Alexa to automatically delete voice recordings after a certain period, providing an added layer of control over your data.

Another privacy measure that Amazon has implemented is the ability to control what Alexa "remembers." With Alexa Plus's advanced memory function, the assistant can recall important information about your preferences, dietary restrictions, and routines. While this feature can be incredibly helpful in personalizing your experience, it also comes with the potential for privacy concerns. To address this, Amazon gives you full control over the memory function. You can review and delete specific memories, and Alexa will notify you whenever it updates or recalls information, ensuring that you're always aware of what's being stored.

Amazon has also made it easier for users to disable certain features if they prefer a more limited experience. For instance, you can disable voice recording altogether, preventing Alexa from storing any spoken commands. Additionally, you can turn off certain integrations, such as the ability to control your smart home devices, if you're uncomfortable with how Alexa is interacting with your environment. These customizable privacy settings allow you to strike the right balance between enjoying the benefits of Alexa's advanced features while maintaining control over your personal information.

The integration of third-party services through Alexa also raises questions about how much personal data is shared beyond Amazon's ecosystem. While Alexa can connect with external platforms like OpenTable, Spotify, and more, Amazon emphasizes that they are committed to maintaining the same level of privacy and security across all integrations. Alexa Plus will only share necessary data with third-party services and will adhere to strict data protection policies. Additionally, users can manage these integrations and limit the amount of data shared with external partners through the Alexa app's privacy settings.

Despite these protections, it's important to understand that no system is entirely free from risks. Users must remain vigilant and proactive in managing their privacy settings. While Alexa Plus offers powerful tools for securing your data, ultimately, how much information you choose to share and store with Alexa is in your hands.

In a world where data privacy is an ever-growing concern, Amazon's approach to securing Alexa Plus reflects the company's commitment to user protection. By prioritizing encryption, local processing, and offering transparency through the privacy dashboard, Amazon aims to reassure users that their personal data remains safe while still delivering the powerful capabilities that make Alexa Plus such an indispensable tool. As Alexa becomes more integrated into our homes and daily routines, users will need to continue to educate themselves on the evolving privacy landscape and take the necessary steps to safeguard their information.

Ultimately, the balance between convenience and privacy is a personal decision for each user. Amazon has made significant efforts to mitigate privacy risks and offer control to the user, but it's important to remain aware of how the assistant works and actively manage your settings. By doing so, Alexa

Plus can be a helpful, secure, and personalized tool in your smart home.

Chapter 5: Alexa Plus for Everyday Use – Helping with the Little Things

Alexa Plus has transformed the way we approach everyday tasks, offering a level of convenience that makes it feel like a natural extension of our daily lives. Gone are the days when we only used Alexa to ask simple questions like, "What's the weather today?" or "Set a timer for 10 minutes." While these basic functions are still a core part of Alexa's capabilities, Alexa Plus has evolved into a more robust assistant, effortlessly managing a wide range of activities—both simple and complex.

At its core, Alexa Plus handles the tasks that many of us rely on daily without breaking a sweat. You can still ask Alexa to check the weather, set alarms, or control your smart lights—all of which are now more intuitive and efficient. With the added contextual awareness of Alexa Plus, these tasks feel more natural. For instance, Alexa doesn't just tell you the temperature; it may also provide you with tailored recommendations, like suggesting you wear a coat if it's particularly cold outside or reminding you to grab an umbrella if there's rain in the forecast. These contextual insights add a layer of intelligence that traditional assistants simply couldn't match.

Setting alarms has also become more intuitive. Alexa Plus doesn't just set the time—it now understands the context of your request. For example, if you ask Alexa to wake you up in the morning and mention you need extra time for a meeting, it can adjust the alarm based on your routine. It can even provide a gentle wake-up message to help you start the day on a positive note, enhancing the personal connection and making everyday tasks feel a little bit more thoughtful.

But Alexa Plus doesn't stop at basic tasks. It takes on more advanced use cases, transforming how you interact with your home, schedule, and even research needs. Managing your calendar, for instance, is a breeze with Alexa Plus. If you're juggling a busy week of appointments, it can provide reminders, suggest time slots for meetings, and even help with rescheduling. Gone are the days of manual calendar entries or forgotten events. With just a voice command, Alexa can keep your calendar in check, and because it remembers details about your routine, it can help prevent scheduling conflicts or remind you to prepare for upcoming appointments.

When it comes to controlling your smart home, Alexa Plus is truly in a league of its own. Whether it's adjusting the thermostat, controlling the lights, or managing the security system, Alexa now understands the nuances of your preferences and can make decisions on your behalf. For example, if you usually dim the lights in the evening for a movie night, Alexa Plus will remember this and can automatically adjust the lighting when you say, "Alexa, start movie night." Additionally, with the ability to control third-party devices from various manufacturers, Alexa Plus creates a seamless experience where multiple smart home gadgets work together in harmony.

Alexa Plus has also become a powerful tool for research. You can now ask it to perform more complex research tasks beyond simple questions. If you're planning a trip, Alexa can suggest destinations, look up flight options, and even create itineraries based on your preferences. If you're learning about a particular topic, it can gather information from multiple sources, summarize the most important points, and help you prepare for a conversation or presentation. By leveraging large language models, Alexa is capable of parsing vast amounts of information, organizing it effectively, and delivering it in a format that makes sense to you.

What truly sets Alexa Plus apart from previous versions is the deep integration of AI that allows it to anticipate your needs and perform tasks proactively. If you have a recurring task, like paying bills at the end of the month, Alexa Plus can remind you and even suggest steps to streamline the process, such as automatically pulling up payment methods or reminding you about discounts and offers you might have missed. It's the level of foresight and contextual awareness that transforms Alexa from a passive tool to an active partner in managing your daily life.

As Alexa Plus evolves, it's clear that the assistant isn't just about completing commands—it's about becoming an intelligent part of your life that understands your preferences, anticipates your needs, and helps you manage the complexities of the modern world. Whether it's a simple task like checking the weather or a more advanced function like coordinating your calendar and smart home devices, Alexa Plus is making everyday life easier in ways we never thought possible. As users continue to discover the potential of this advanced assistant, it's safe to say that the days of basic voice commands are long behind us. Alexa Plus is now an indispensable companion in navigating daily life, and its capabilities are only going to grow from here.

Alexa Plus is increasingly becoming an indispensable tool for students and professionals alike, expanding far beyond its original role as a voice assistant. With its enhanced intelligence, Alexa now serves as a powerful study buddy and document assistant, making learning and working more efficient and less stressful.

One of the standout features of Alexa Plus in this context is its ability to interact with documents in a way that was never before possible. Imagine you have a lengthy research paper, a set of meeting notes, or even a stack of study materials for an exam. Instead of sifting through pages of text or opening multiple tabs on your computer, you can simply upload the documents to Alexa and ask it to summarize them for you. Whether you're studying for a final exam or preparing for a big presentation, Alexa Plus can quickly condense complex materials into easily digestible summaries, providing key points and insights within seconds. This time-saving feature allows users to focus on what matters most—whether it's grasping the core concepts of a subject or fine-tuning a project for work.

For students, Alexa Plus can take studying to the next level by offering interactive quizzes and study sessions. Whether you're learning a new language, preparing for a test, or revising for an exam, Alexa Plus can quiz you on the material and provide real-time feedback. Alexa can even adjust the difficulty of the questions based on your progress, ensuring that the study session stays challenging but manageable. This makes it a valuable tool for active learning, where students engage with the content in a dynamic and personalized way, rather than passively reviewing notes or textbooks. Alexa can help reinforce the material by asking follow-up questions, offering explanations, and even providing hints if you're struggling to recall a key concept.

For professionals, Alexa Plus offers similar advantages, turning it into a document assistant that can be used in everyday work scenarios. Need to prepare for a meeting and don't have time to read through the entire report? Just upload the document to Alexa, and it can give you a summary of the most critical points. If you're working on a project and need to reference specific sections of a lengthy report, you can simply ask Alexa to pull up the relevant information. This feature is particularly useful in high-pressure environments where time is of the essence, allowing you to make informed decisions quickly and without getting bogged down by lengthy documents.

Another key aspect of Alexa Plus as a study buddy and document assistant is its integration with other platforms, which makes it even more versatile. For example, you can link Alexa with cloud storage services, making it easy to upload, access, and review documents stored online. If you're working on a research project, Alexa can pull from various sources and help you organize your notes, making sure everything is in one place and easily accessible. It can also cross-reference materials, helping you to find related information and connect the dots between various ideas.

When studying, it's important not only to absorb information but also to retain it. Alexa Plus helps with this by engaging users in active recall exercises. For example, after you review a set of notes, Alexa can ask you questions about the material and track your responses to gauge your retention. If you get an answer wrong, Alexa can offer an explanation or rephrase the question to help reinforce the concept. This adaptive learning process makes Alexa Plus more than just a tool for reading and summarizing; it becomes an active participant in your learning journey.

In addition, Alexa Plus's ability to assist with multitasking is invaluable for students and professionals who often juggle multiple responsibilities. For instance, if you're working on a document while preparing for an exam, Alexa can manage your time by setting reminders, scheduling study breaks, or providing periodic summaries of what you've worked on so far. You can even ask it to set timers for specific tasks, ensuring that you're staying on track without feeling overwhelmed.

Alexa Plus also enables better document organization and retrieval. If you're studying for a test or working on a report, you might have multiple documents to sift through. With Alexa Plus, you can simply ask it to retrieve specific sections of documents or to highlight key terms or concepts. This makes it an ideal tool for students who are working with dense, academic material, as well as for professionals who need to quickly reference large amounts of text during meetings or presentations.

For students preparing for exams, the interactive nature of Alexa Plus makes it an ideal tool for flashcard-style learning. Alexa can quiz you on terms, dates, formulas, or concepts from your study materials, offering feedback as you go. It can even repeat questions or ask them in different ways to ensure that you truly understand the material. This level of personalized, on-demand interaction makes Alexa Plus an ideal companion for active studying and review sessions.

As students and professionals continue to rely more heavily on digital tools to stay organized and efficient, Alexa Plus's ability to assist with document management, studying, and research tasks is a game-changer. Whether it's summarizing long texts, quizzing on complex topics, or helping you stay organized, Alexa Plus is more than just a voice assistant—it's a proactive learning and productivity partner. As its capabilities expand, Alexa Plus will undoubtedly become an even more invaluable tool in the worlds of education and professional development, empowering users to do more with less effort and helping them succeed in their respective fields.

Chapter 6: The Future of Alexa – What's Next for AI and Personal Assistance

Alexa Plus is increasingly becoming an indispensable tool for students and professionals alike, expanding far beyond its original role as a voice assistant. With its enhanced intelligence, Alexa now serves as a powerful study buddy and document assistant, making learning and working more efficient and less stressful.

One of the standout features of Alexa Plus in this context is its ability to interact with documents in a way that was never before possible. Imagine you have a lengthy research paper, a set of meeting notes, or even a stack of study materials for an exam. Instead of sifting through pages of text or opening multiple tabs on your computer, you can simply upload the documents to Alexa and ask it to summarize them for you. Whether you're studying for a final exam or preparing for a big presentation, Alexa Plus can quickly condense complex materials into easily digestible summaries, providing key points and insights within seconds. This time-saving feature allows users to focus on what matters most—whether it's grasping the core concepts of a subject or fine-tuning a project for work.

For students, Alexa Plus can take studying to the next level by offering interactive quizzes and study sessions. Whether you're learning a new language, preparing for a test, or revising for an exam, Alexa Plus can quiz you on the material and provide real-time feedback. Alexa can even adjust the difficulty of the questions based on your progress, ensuring that the study session stays challenging but manageable. This makes it a valuable tool for active learning, where students engage with the content in a dynamic and personalized way, rather than passively reviewing notes or textbooks. Alexa can help reinforce the material by asking follow-up questions, offering explanations, and even providing hints if you're struggling to recall a key concept.

For professionals, Alexa Plus offers similar advantages, turning it into a document assistant that can be used in everyday work scenarios. Need to prepare for a meeting and don't have time to read through the entire report? Just upload the document to Alexa, and it can give you a summary of the most critical points. If you're working on a project and need to reference specific sections of a lengthy report, you can simply ask Alexa to pull up the relevant information. This feature is particularly useful in high-pressure environments where time is of the essence, allowing you to make informed decisions quickly and without getting bogged down by lengthy documents.

Another key aspect of Alexa Plus as a study buddy and document assistant is its integration with other platforms, which makes it even more versatile. For example, you can link Alexa with cloud storage services, making it easy to upload, access, and review documents stored online. If you're working on a research project, Alexa can pull from various sources and help you organize your notes, making sure everything is in one place and easily accessible. It can also cross-reference materials, helping you to find related information and connect the dots between various ideas.

When studying, it's important not only to absorb information but also to retain it. Alexa Plus helps with this by engaging users in active recall exercises. For example, after you review a set of notes, Alexa can ask you questions about the material and track your responses to gauge your retention. If you get an answer wrong, Alexa can offer an explanation or rephrase the question to help reinforce the concept. This adaptive learning process makes Alexa Plus more than just a tool for reading and summarizing; it becomes an active participant in your learning journey.

In addition, Alexa Plus's ability to assist with multitasking is invaluable for students and professionals who often juggle multiple responsibilities. For instance, if you're working on a document while preparing for an exam, Alexa can manage your time by setting reminders, scheduling study breaks, or providing periodic summaries of what you've worked on so far. You can even ask it to set timers for specific tasks, ensuring that you're staying on track without feeling overwhelmed.

Alexa Plus also enables better document organization and retrieval. If you're studying for a test or working on a report, you might have multiple documents to sift through. With Alexa Plus, you can simply ask it to retrieve specific sections of documents or to highlight key terms or concepts. This makes it an ideal tool for students who are working with dense, academic material, as well as for professionals who need to quickly reference large amounts of text during meetings or presentations.

For students preparing for exams, the interactive nature of Alexa Plus makes it an ideal tool for flashcard-style learning. Alexa can quiz you on terms, dates, formulas, or concepts from your study materials, offering feedback as you go. It can even repeat questions or ask them in different ways to ensure that you truly understand the material. This level of personalized, on-demand interaction makes Alexa Plus an ideal companion for active studying and review sessions.

As students and professionals continue to rely more heavily on digital tools to stay organized and efficient, Alexa Plus's ability to assist with document management, studying, and research tasks is a game-changer. Whether it's summarizing long texts, quizzing on complex topics, or helping you stay organized, Alexa Plus is more than just a voice assistant—it's a proactive learning and productivity partner. As its capabilities expand, Alexa Plus will undoubtedly become an even more invaluable tool in the worlds of education and professional development, empowering users to do more with less effort and helping them succeed in their respective fields.

The role of Alexa in the global market is poised for significant expansion as Amazon positions Alexa Plus at the forefront of the evolving personal assistance and smart home technology sectors. With its groundbreaking integration of generative AI and large language models, Alexa Plus is not just another upgrade; it's a leap forward in the way consumers interact with technology. As the digital landscape becomes increasingly connected, Alexa Plus offers an unprecedented opportunity for Amazon to dominate the future of AI-powered devices, providing a seamless, personalized experience for users worldwide.

Amazon's early foray into voice assistants with the original Alexa has already reshaped how we interact with smart home devices, bringing voice recognition and automation to millions of households. Alexa's ability to control smart gadgets, manage daily tasks, and provide real-time information has made it a core component of countless homes. However, with the introduction of

Alexa Plus, Amazon is aiming to elevate the voice assistant into something far more sophisticated—an intelligent, context-aware assistant capable of understanding and anticipating user needs in a way that was previously unthinkable.

The global market for AI-powered personal assistants and smart home devices is growing at an exponential rate, with industry projections suggesting that the smart home market will reach over $200 billion by the late 2020s. In this competitive landscape, Amazon is positioning Alexa Plus not only to compete but to lead the charge. The integration of advanced AI capabilities, such as conversational memory, personalized suggestions, and multi-step task handling, allows Alexa Plus to provide a richer, more engaging user experience compared to its predecessors. This evolution of Alexa opens up new possibilities for how consumers interact with their homes, their personal data, and their day-to-day lives, placing Alexa Plus at the heart of the emerging AI-driven lifestyle.

One of the key areas where Alexa Plus could change the global landscape is its potential to redefine the concept of a personal assistant. Until now, virtual assistants like Siri, Google Assistant, and Alexa have largely been limited to responding to specific voice commands and providing information. However, Alexa Plus, powered by Claude from Anthropic and Amazon's own AI technologies, leverages the power of generative AI to move beyond mere command execution. This allows Alexa to engage in deeper, more complex interactions with users, providing assistance in ways that were not previously possible. Whether it's managing schedules, offering tailored recommendations, or making real-time decisions based on contextual data, Alexa Plus is shifting the paradigm of what a virtual assistant can do, setting new standards for the entire industry.

As Amazon pushes forward with Alexa Plus, the company faces intense competition from other tech giants like Google, Apple, and Microsoft. Each of these companies is making its own strides in AI development, particularly in the realm of voice assistants and smart home technologies. Google's Assistant, for instance, has made significant progress in understanding natural language and context, while Apple has consistently focused on privacy and seamless integration with its ecosystem. However, Amazon's advantage lies in its extensive reach, from its e-commerce dominance to its cloud computing arm, AWS, and now its home automation leadership with Alexa. With Alexa Plus, Amazon is looking to solidify its position not just as a player in the voice assistant market, but as a leader in the next wave of AI-powered personal assistance.

The strategic importance of Alexa Plus extends far beyond Amazon's core business of e-commerce and cloud computing. The success of Alexa Plus will have a direct impact on the company's ability to capture and retain consumer attention, creating new opportunities for revenue generation. For example, the integration of Alexa with third-party services, such as grocery deliveries, restaurant reservations, and entertainment, creates a powerful ecosystem where users are incentivized to remain within the Amazon environment. In addition, Alexa's ability to handle tasks ranging from basic home automation to complex decision-making opens the door for new subscription-based services, premium features, and data-driven offerings that could generate significant revenue streams.

In the global market, Alexa Plus represents a compelling opportunity for Amazon to extend its reach into emerging markets where smart home adoption is still in its infancy. As internet access and mobile device penetration continue to grow in regions like Asia, Africa, and Latin America, the demand for AI-powered personal assistants is expected to surge. Alexa's relatively low-cost Echo devices, combined with the advanced capabilities of Alexa Plus, make it an attractive solution for consumers in these regions looking to adopt smart home technologies. Furthermore, Amazon's established global logistics network ensures that Alexa Plus can be delivered to virtually any corner of the globe, allowing the company to tap into new customer bases that may have previously been inaccessible.

The potential of Alexa's growth, especially in the context of competing tech giants, is immense. As the industry continues to evolve, companies will increasingly rely on AI technologies to drive innovation and deliver new value to customers. With Alexa Plus leading the way, Amazon is not just participating in this revolution—it is driving it. As more users experience the transformative capabilities of Alexa Plus, it could set the standard for what the next generation of personal assistants and smart home devices should look like, and in doing so, redefine the future of human-technology interaction.

In a world where artificial intelligence is rapidly becoming an integral part of our daily lives, Alexa

Plus stands out as a symbol of what's possible when AI is combined with seamless integration and personalized experiences. As Amazon continues to refine its AI capabilities and expand its global reach, Alexa Plus will undoubtedly play a pivotal role in shaping the future of smart homes, personal assistance, and digital interaction in ways we can only begin to imagine.

Chapter 7: Pricing and Availability – What You Need to Know

The cost of Alexa Plus is one of the critical factors that will determine its accessibility and appeal to a wide range of users. Amazon has strategically designed its pricing structure to cater to both Prime and non-Prime customers, ensuring that it remains competitive in the increasingly crowded market of smart home devices and personal assistants.

For Amazon Prime members, the cost of Alexa Plus is typically bundled with additional perks, reflecting the company's commitment to making its ecosystem even more attractive to existing subscribers. Prime members, who already enjoy benefits such as free shipping, streaming services, and exclusive deals, will find that Alexa Plus is offered at a discounted price or with added features included as part of their membership. This move encourages Amazon's loyal customer base to upgrade to the new assistant without feeling the financial strain that comes with purchasing standalone devices. For many Prime users, Alexa Plus becomes an easy, value-driven upgrade that further integrates them into the Amazon ecosystem.

For non-Prime users, Alexa Plus will likely come with a slightly higher price tag, reflecting the additional costs of offering the service to a broader audience. While Amazon hasn't officially released a final pricing structure, it's expected that Alexa Plus will be priced similarly to or slightly higher than the existing Alexa devices, depending on the model and capabilities. This pricing will still be competitive in comparison to other smart assistants on the market, with Amazon likely offering various tiers of Alexa Plus devices depending on features like sound quality, display size, and additional smart home functionalities.

In addition to the core pricing structure, Amazon is also offering an early access program for Alexa Plus. This program is aimed at generating interest and excitement around the launch of Alexa Plus, giving customers the chance to try out the new features and functionalities before they are available to the general public. Early access typically comes with a few benefits: users get a chance to experience Alexa Plus at a reduced price, potentially as part of a limited-time offer, and they also have the opportunity to provide feedback that could shape future updates and features.

Participants in the early access program can expect a more direct and personalized experience, often with exclusive features or access to beta testing of upcoming functions. Early access is an excellent way for Amazon to build buzz around Alexa Plus, generating word-of-mouth marketing from tech enthusiasts, early adopters, and existing Alexa users. For users looking to get Alexa Plus as soon as possible, signing up for this program ensures they don't miss out on the chance to experience the next-gen assistant first. It also allows them to enjoy all of the exciting new features that Alexa Plus offers at a fraction of the eventual retail cost.

This tiered pricing model and early access program are designed to make Alexa Plus as accessible as possible to a wide variety of users, from long-time Prime subscribers to those who are just starting to explore the world of smart home technology. While the exact cost remains to be seen, it's clear that Amazon is positioning Alexa Plus as a game-changer for both its loyal customers and a broader audience, ensuring that more people can integrate advanced AI into their everyday lives without breaking the bank.

Not every device is built to handle the level of intelligence that Alexa Plus brings to the table. While Amazon has worked hard to ensure widespread accessibility, only certain Echo models are equipped with the necessary processing power to support the new AI-driven assistant. Users with newer Echo devices will be able to experience the full range of Alexa Plus's features, while those with older models will have to stick with the standard Alexa experience.

The latest Echo Show models, including the Echo Show 8 (3rd Gen), Echo Show 10, and Echo Show 15, are among the devices that can run Alexa Plus. These models are designed with advanced hardware that allows for deeper contextual awareness, better conversational flow, and improved memory capabilities. The Echo Hub, a newer addition to Amazon's smart home lineup, is also fully compatible, making it a great choice for those who want a central control system for their home automation. For users who already own these devices, Alexa Plus will be accessible with a simple software update.

However, not all Echo devices are equipped to support the upgrade. The first-generation Echo Dot, Echo Spot, and early Echo Show models won't be able to handle Alexa Plus due to hardware limitations. These older models will continue functioning with the standard Alexa voice assistant, meaning they will still perform basic tasks like setting timers, checking the weather, and controlling smart home devices, but without the advanced AI-driven personalization and memory features. Amazon has yet to announce whether it will release a version of Alexa Plus optimized for older hardware, but for now, upgrading to a newer model is the only way to access the full capabilities.

Beyond Echo devices, Alexa Plus is designed to work across a variety of platforms, making it more versatile than ever. Fire TV devices are a key part of this ecosystem, allowing users to interact with Alexa Plus while browsing content, receiving AI-powered recommendations, and managing home automation from their television screen. This integration makes it easy to control entertainment and smart home functions in one place, giving users a hands-free way to access information and manage daily tasks.

For those who rely on Fire Tablets, Alexa Plus extends its functionality to these devices, making it easier to stay connected to the assistant even while reading, browsing, or working. Fire Tablets serve as an additional access point for Alexa Plus, offering both voice control and touchscreen interactions for those who prefer a more visual interface. This makes it ideal for users who want to review summaries, manage documents, or handle research tasks in a more interactive way.

Mobile users aren't left out either. The Alexa app on iOS and Android has been updated to support Alexa Plus, allowing users to access their assistant on the go. This means you can start a conversation with Alexa at home on an Echo device, then continue the interaction on your phone while driving or walking. This cross-device functionality ensures a seamless experience, with Alexa Plus maintaining memory and context across different platforms. Whether you're setting reminders, checking your schedule, or adjusting smart home settings remotely, the mobile app ensures that Alexa Plus is always within reach.

For those who prefer working on a larger screen, Alexa Plus is also available through Alexa.com, where users can interact with their assistant from a desktop or laptop. This feature is particularly useful for professionals who need document summaries, research assistance, or schedule management while working. The ability to switch between devices without losing context makes Alexa Plus a truly integrated assistant that adapts to various lifestyles and work habits.

With its broad compatibility across Echo devices, Fire TV, Fire Tablets, mobile apps, and web browsers, Alexa Plus is designed to fit seamlessly into the way users live and work. Whether at home or on the go, the assistant remains accessible, intelligent, and always ready to assist. For those who want the full AI-powered experience, upgrading to a supported Echo device or using Alexa Plus through its extended platforms will unlock its full potential, making it more than just a voice assistant—it becomes an integral part of daily life.

Chapter 8: The Pros and Cons of Alexa Plus – Is It Worth the Price?

Alexa Plus represents a major leap forward in AI-powered personal assistance, making everyday interactions feel more natural, intelligent, and intuitive. The upgrades go far beyond simple command-and-response functions, turning Alexa into an assistant that not only listens but understands, remembers, and adapts to your needs over time. With more conversational depth, better integration across devices, and a high level of personalization, Alexa Plus offers users an experience that is tailored to their lifestyle, making it a valuable addition to any smart home.

One of the most noticeable improvements with Alexa Plus is how much smarter and more conversational it has become. Unlike the traditional Alexa, which could sometimes feel robotic or limited in its ability to follow conversations, Alexa Plus has the power of generative AI behind it. This means that interactions flow more naturally—Alexa can recall details from previous discussions, understand context, and respond in a way that feels more human-like. Instead of giving one-off answers to questions, it can now follow up, clarify requests, and provide more meaningful suggestions. If you mention you're planning a trip, for example, Alexa Plus won't just give you weather updates for your destination—it might also remind you to pack based on your previous travel habits, suggest nearby restaurants that fit your dietary preferences, and even help you book transportation. The ability to hold a conversation rather than just execute commands makes it feel less like a machine and more like an intuitive, helpful companion.

Another major advantage of Alexa Plus is its deeper integration with smart devices and third-party services. While the original Alexa was already a powerful tool for controlling smart home gadgets, Alexa Plus takes this to another level by working more intelligently across multiple devices. Whether it's adjusting lighting based on your routines, setting the perfect temperature before you arrive home, or monitoring security cameras in real time, Alexa Plus ensures that your smart home setup is not just responsive, but proactive. Integrations with Ring security systems allow for hands-free home monitoring, while Fire TV support means you can receive personalized entertainment recommendations based on your watching habits. Alexa Plus also connects seamlessly with services like OpenTable for reservations, Spotify and Amazon Music for curated playlists, and even food delivery platforms, making everyday tasks as effortless as a simple voice command.

But what truly sets Alexa Plus apart is its ability to personalize experiences based on contextual awareness. Unlike traditional voice assistants that treat each request as an isolated command, Alexa Plus remembers details about your preferences, habits, and daily life. If you frequently order a morning coffee through a delivery app, Alexa Plus might remind you when you forget or suggest a new drink based on past orders. If you're someone who prefers waking up to soft instrumental music instead of an alarm, Alexa can make that adjustment automatically, learning and adapting over time. This level of personalization extends to multiple aspects of daily life, from meal recommendations that align with your dietary restrictions to fitness reminders that help keep you on track with your goals.

Contextual understanding also allows Alexa Plus to provide multi-step assistance without requiring constant clarification. If you say, "Alexa, I'm planning a dinner party," it won't just suggest recipes—it will help you create a grocery list, check your pantry inventory, suggest a playlist for the evening, and even send out invitations if needed. The assistant recognizes the broader intent behind your request and proactively takes steps to make the process smoother. This is a fundamental shift from the traditional voice assistant experience, where users had to issue multiple individual commands to accomplish a task.

These improvements collectively make Alexa Plus not just an assistant, but a deeply integrated part of your daily routine. With smarter conversations, seamless smart home control, and an unparalleled level of personalization, Alexa Plus has transformed what a virtual assistant can be, offering a highly responsive and intuitive experience that adapts to the way you live.

While Alexa Plus offers an impressive set of features that take virtual assistance to a new level, it's not without its drawbacks. For all its intelligence and seamless integration, there are some key concerns that may make potential users hesitant to upgrade. Whether it's the cost, privacy implications, or questions about its real-world performance, Alexa Plus comes with trade-offs that every user needs to consider before deciding if it's truly worth it.

One of the most debated aspects of Alexa Plus is its pricing model. While Prime members get access at no extra cost, non-Prime users will have to pay $19.99 per month to use the upgraded assistant. For many, this feels like a significant jump from the free version of Alexa that they've grown accustomed to using for years. The question then becomes: Is it worth the price?

For users who are deeply invested in the Amazon ecosystem—those who rely on Alexa for smart home control, personal assistance, and entertainment—the subscription may feel justified. The enhanced conversational abilities, contextual awareness, and proactive task management offer clear benefits that could save time and effort. However, for those who only use Alexa for occasional commands, checking the weather, or controlling a few smart home devices, the additional cost may not seem worthwhile. It raises the concern that Amazon is moving Alexa towards a paywall model, where the best features are locked behind a subscription, forcing users to either pay or stick with the more basic version.

Privacy has always been a point of concern with voice assistants, but Alexa Plus takes data collection to a deeper level. With the ability to remember personal details, track routines, and store user preferences over time, some may wonder: How much data is too much? The idea of an AI assistant that "remembers" conversations and anticipates needs is undeniably useful, but it also means that Amazon has access to more information about users than ever before. While the company claims that Alexa Plus prioritizes security with encryption and local processing, the reality is that much of this data still passes through Amazon's servers.

For privacy-conscious individuals, the thought of a voice assistant collecting long-term behavioral data raises red flags. Even with Amazon's privacy dashboard allowing users to review and delete stored interactions, there's an underlying concern about how much control users actually have over their data. Some may worry about potential third-party integrations and whether their personal preferences, shopping habits, or even security camera footage could be used for advertising or other business strategies. While Amazon insists that user data is protected, skepticism remains, especially in an era where digital privacy concerns are more relevant than ever.

Beyond pricing and privacy, another major question looms: Will Alexa Plus live up to the hype? While the promise of an advanced AI-driven assistant sounds exciting, real-world performance will ultimately determine its success. Early reports from demos suggest that Alexa Plus still has moments where it misunderstands context, gives inaccurate responses, or requires repeated prompts to complete tasks correctly. Generative AI is powerful, but it's not perfect. The risk of AI "hallucinations," where the system generates incorrect or misleading information, is a well-known issue with large language models. If Alexa Plus suffers from similar problems, users may find themselves frustrated rather than impressed by its abilities.

Another concern is technical reliability. As Alexa Plus integrates with more third-party services and smart home devices, the complexity of its interactions increases. If something goes wrong—whether it's a delayed response, an error in execution, or a misunderstanding of user intent—it could disrupt the experience rather than enhance it. Users who have relied on Alexa for years may find it jarring if the new AI-driven assistant introduces inconsistencies or requires constant corrections.

Ultimately, while Alexa Plus brings undeniable advancements in AI-driven personal assistance, it's not a flawless upgrade. The subscription cost could alienate non-Prime users, the privacy concerns may make some hesitant to embrace its deeper level of personalization, and technical reliability remains an open question. Whether Alexa Plus is worth the investment depends on how much users are willing to trade off between convenience, privacy, and cost.

As the technology evolves, Amazon will need to address these concerns to ensure that Alexa Plus truly becomes the next-generation assistant it promises to be.

Chapter 9: A Look at the Competitors – How Does Alexa Plus Stack Up?

In the rapidly evolving world of smart assistants, Alexa Plus is not entering an empty space. It's competing against other major players like Google Assistant, Apple's Siri, and various other AI-driven technologies that promise to simplify tasks, answer questions, and control our homes. But what sets Alexa Plus apart? How does it measure up against these established assistants, and what makes it unique in an increasingly crowded marketplace?

Google Assistant has long been regarded as one of the most intelligent voice assistants on the market, especially when it comes to understanding natural language and handling complex queries. Google's integration with its vast search engine capabilities allows Google Assistant to provide answers to a wide variety of questions—sometimes even outperforming Alexa when it comes to knowledge-based queries. Additionally, Google has a strong presence in the smart home space through

Nest devices, offering seamless control over thermostats, cameras, and lights.

However, Alexa Plus takes things a step further in terms of contextual understanding and personalization. While Google Assistant excels at answering questions, Alexa Plus is designed to create a more nuanced, interactive experience. Alexa can store long-term information about users' routines, preferences, and specific needs, something that Google Assistant has only recently started experimenting with. Alexa Plus's integration with large language models allows it to remember conversations and anticipate future needs—providing a more human-like interaction. Whether it's remembering your partner's dietary restrictions or suggesting recipes based on your previous preferences, Alexa Plus offers a level of personalized service that sets it apart.

When it comes to Apple's Siri, the comparison is a bit more complicated. Siri has always been closely integrated with Apple's ecosystem, which is both a strength and a limitation. For Apple users, Siri works seamlessly with iPhones, iPads, Macs, and other Apple devices. However, the experience of interacting with Siri can feel somewhat rigid and scripted compared to Alexa Plus. Siri tends to offer shorter responses and lacks the level of proactive interaction that Alexa Plus provides. Siri's lack of cross-platform compatibility (for example, it doesn't support non-Apple smart devices) also limits its potential compared to Alexa, which works well with a broad range of third-party devices through the Alexa app and Echo devices.

Alexa Plus, with its deeper integration with smart home gadgets, third-party services like OpenTable, and even shopping assistance, provides a broader, more versatile user experience. In particular, the ability to leverage generative AI for memory and personalized recommendations gives Alexa a cutting edge in terms of anticipating needs. Siri, while competent, lacks this level of personalization and often doesn't remember user preferences as well as Alexa Plus does.

As for other smart assistants on the market, such as Samsung's Bixby or various lesser-known options, they still trail far behind in terms of AI sophistication and personalization. Bixby tries to integrate with Samsung's ecosystem but doesn't have the broad third-party support or memory capabilities that Alexa Plus has. Furthermore, none of these assistants have yet integrated large language models to the extent that Alexa Plus has, which allows for more natural conversations and a deeper understanding of user context.

The unique selling point of Alexa Plus lies in its AI-driven personalization and contextual awareness. By utilizing Claude AI from Anthropic and Amazon's Bedrock platform, Alexa Plus is able to build on the foundation of Amazon's ecosystem of smart home devices, making it not just a virtual assistant, but a highly intelligent partner in everyday life. The ability to remember specific details, anticipate needs, and handle complex, proactive tasks like making reservations or suggesting grocery lists makes Alexa Plus a more dynamic and interactive assistant compared to its competitors.

While Google Assistant may still edge out Alexa in terms of search capabilities, and Siri may offer a smoother experience within the Apple ecosystem, Alexa Plus has redefined the standard for what a smart assistant can do. Its ability to integrate deeply with smart home devices, remember user preferences, and facilitate complex, context-driven conversations gives it an edge in a competitive market. Alexa Plus doesn't just respond—it learns, adapts, and offers a truly personalized experience that keeps users engaged and invested.

What sets Alexa Plus apart from other virtual assistants is the integration of cutting-edge AI technologies, specifically Claude, a powerful AI model developed by Anthropic, and Amazon's proprietary AI capabilities through its Bedrock platform. This combination marks a significant shift in how Alexa interacts with users, setting it apart from the competition in several key ways.

At its core, Claude provides Alexa Plus with a level of contextual understanding and conversational memory that previous iterations of Alexa, or any other smart assistant for that matter, simply couldn't match. Unlike other assistants that rely on pre-programmed responses or short-term interactions, Claude enables Alexa to engage in ongoing conversations, remember past exchanges, and anticipate your future needs. For instance, if you've told Alexa about your daily routine, your dietary preferences, or even your weekend plans, Alexa Plus can recall those details and tailor its responses accordingly. This ongoing memory allows Alexa to provide highly personalized suggestions, such as recommending recipes, planning events, or even assisting with shopping lists based on past interactions.

What's truly remarkable about Claude's integration is its ability to understand nuances in conversation that go beyond basic commands. It enables deeper, more meaningful interactions, meaning that Alexa can offer more than just answers—it can engage in dynamic, context-aware conversations. If you're having a chat about your plans for the day, Alexa might remember previous conversations about your favorite restaurants, specific events, or even your travel preferences, providing insights or recommendations without you having to ask explicitly. This level of personalization creates an experience that feels much more human and less mechanical.

But it's not just Claude that makes Alexa Plus stand out. Amazon's Bedrock platform is another defining feature that enhances Alexa's capabilities. Bedrock serves as Amazon's backbone for AI and machine learning, allowing Alexa to tap into vast amounts of data and powerful generative AI models for a broader, more adaptive performance. Through this platform, Alexa can process and analyze information in real-time, making its responses not only faster but also more accurate and tailored to each user's unique needs.

Together, Claude and Bedrock create an environment where Alexa Plus doesn't just respond to commands—it learns, adapts, and grows over time. This ability to remember, anticipate, and contextualize makes Alexa Plus far more intelligent than its predecessors or competitors. It moves away from the traditional, task-oriented assistant role and enters the realm of a true personal partner in daily life, capable of handling a wide variety of tasks, offering personalized suggestions, and maintaining a long-term relationship with users.

This evolutionary leap in AI integration also positions Alexa Plus as an ideal candidate for the smart home of the future. As Amazon continues to refine and expand the capabilities of its AI technologies, Alexa Plus is poised to become more than just an assistant—it will become an integral part of users' lives, managing everything from smart devices to scheduling, shopping, and even family interactions.

In essence, what sets Alexa Plus apart from other virtual assistants is the sophisticated use of Claude's memory capabilities, Bedrock's AI infrastructure, and the deep integration of both into Amazon's broader ecosystem of smart devices. It's not just about controlling your smart home anymore; it's about creating an assistant that understands you, anticipates your needs, and grows smarter with you over time.

Conclusion

As technology continues to evolve, the role of artificial intelligence in our daily lives is becoming more profound and integrated. The advancement of AI-powered personal assistants, like Alexa Plus, signals a pivotal shift in how we manage tasks, interact with our homes, and navigate the world around us. Where once we relied on simple voice commands and static routines, Alexa Plus takes this to the next level by offering dynamic, personalized experiences that adapt to the user's needs in real-time.

The leap forward that Alexa Plus represents goes beyond just improving existing features. It introduces a level of contextual awareness and conversational memory that makes interacting with Alexa more like conversing with a personal assistant who truly understands you. Whether it's remembering your preferences, offering contextual suggestions, or helping to organize your day seamlessly, Alexa Plus redefines the experience of having a smart assistant in the home. The integration of Claude and Amazon's Bedrock platform ensures that Alexa Plus is capable of tackling more complex tasks with ease, making the whole experience feel fluid and intuitive.

In many ways, Alexa Plus is at the forefront of a new era in personal assistance, where AI moves beyond being a passive tool and instead becomes an active partner in your daily life. With deeper integration into smart homes, personalized interactions, and even real-time memory of your preferences, Alexa is now positioned to be a true companion, helping manage everything from home security to entertainment and meal planning. It is no longer just about executing commands—it's about creating a smarter, more connected environment that evolves with you.

For many, Alexa Plus has the potential to revolutionize not only how we interact with our homes but also how we manage our schedules, make decisions, and automate everyday tasks. The ability to use generative AI for contextual understanding and memory means that Alexa can foresee needs, make proactive suggestions, and offer a level of personalized service that was once reserved for the realm of science fiction. In the world of AI assistants, this kind of depth and intelligence positions Alexa Plus as a game-changer.

However, as with all innovations, there are considerations to be made. While Alexa Plus offers immense potential, it's important to recognize that the subscription cost may be a barrier for some users, especially those without a Prime membership. At $19.99 per month, users need to weigh the value of the service against their actual usage and the potential for long-term benefits. In addition, privacy concerns remain a point of discussion, particularly with the deeper integration of AI into daily routines. How much data is being stored, how it is being used, and how protected it is will be a consideration for users who prioritize security.

Finally, while Alexa Plus can transform the way certain individuals interact with their homes and tasks, it may not be necessary for everyone. Those who are looking for a more basic, task-oriented assistant may not need the full capabilities of Alexa Plus. However, for tech enthusiasts, smart home aficionados, or busy individuals looking for a more intelligent and adaptable assistant, Alexa Plus could be the ultimate tool to make daily life more efficient, connected, and enjoyable.

In conclusion, the future of personal assistance looks increasingly AI-driven, and Alexa Plus stands as a beacon of what's possible when technology evolves to become more in tune with our lives. Whether or not it's the right fit for you depends on your needs and how much value you place on having a highly personalized, intelligent assistant at your side. For many, the investment in Alexa Plus could be a step toward a more intuitive and connected future, where artificial intelligence doesn't just support daily tasks, but enhances and enriches the way we live.

www.ingramcontent.com/pod-product-compliance
Lightning Source LLC
LaVergne TN
LVHW051709050326
832903LV00032B/4101